*21st Century Skills* **INNOVATION** *Library*

# Transplants

*by Susan H. Gray*

Published in the United States of America by Cherry Lake Publishing
Ann Arbor, Michigan
www.cherrylakepublishing.com

Content Adviser: Noshene Ranjbar, MD

Design: The Design Lab

Photo Credits: Cover and page 3, ©Peter Jordan/Alamy; page 4, ©Pictorial Press Ltd/Alamy;
pages 6, 9, and 23, ©Mary Evans Picture Library/Alamy; page 11, ©Matthew Collingwood,
used under license from Shutterstock, Inc.; page 12, ©The Print Collector/Alamy; page 14,
©Scott Camazine/Alamy; page 16, ©Sebastian Kaulitzki, used under license from Shutterstock,
Inc.; page 19, ©AP Photo/Al Hartmann, Pool; page 21, ©iStockphoto.com/drbueller; page 25,
©Alvaro Pantoja, used under license from Shutterstock, Inc.; page 26, ©AP Photo; page 28, ©AP
Photo/Bill Veder

Library of Congress Cataloging-in-Publication Data
Gray, Susan Heinrichs
 Transplants / by Susan H. Gray.
    p. cm.–(Innovation in medicine)
 Includes index.
 ISBN-13: 978-1-60279-225-8
 ISBN-10: 1-60279-225-9
 1. Transplantation of organs, tissues, etc.–Juvenile literature.
I. Title. II. Series.
 RD120.76.G73 2009
 617.9'54–dc22                                        2008002583

Cherry Lake Publishing would like to acknowledge the work of
The Partnership for 21st Century Skills.
Please visit www.21stcenturyskills.org for more information.

# CONTENTS

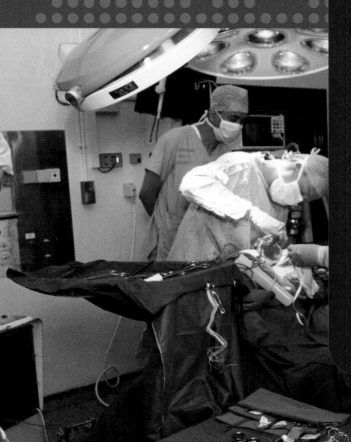

# CHAPTER ONE

# History and Mystery

This is a poster for the movie *Frankenstein*. Today's transplants are nothing like those used for the monster!

The family room was dark except for the light of the TV. Tom and his big brother Jack were watching an old black-and-white movie. Suddenly, the face of Boris Karloff, as Frankenstein's monster, filled the screen. Tom let out a small yelp and dropped his popcorn.

"Scared you, did he?" Jack asked with a laugh.

"Well, yeah," Tom answered. "I guess building a creature from old body parts is never a good idea."

"Probably not," said Jack. "But it's amazing what doctors have done over the years. These days, lots of people's lives are saved with transplants. Doctors weren't always so good at it. But they figured out how to make it work."

Then Jack, the medical student, started to explain.

✼ ✼ ✼

For centuries, surgeons have experimented with human transplants. In these operations, they removed injured or diseased **tissues** or organs and replaced them with healthy ones. Usually, the experiments ended in failure. The most fortunate patients died within minutes of their operations. The unlucky ones dragged on for days, suffering first one problem then another.

Usually, the surgeon performing the transplant had no idea why one patient lived and the next one died. Only in the last 100 years have scientists begun to solve this mystery.

The earliest known transplants took place in India more than 2,500 years ago. At the time, nose **mutilation** was the penalty for theft and other crimes. After receiving their punishment, criminals could not bear to show their faces in public. They sought help from potters and tile makers who could repair their damaged faces. These craftsmen took a slice of flesh from elsewhere on the criminal's body and applied it to the injured area. Some of the subjects healed—probably with rather ugly noses—and went on with their lives.

Without written records, no one knows exactly what kinds of transplants were attempted over the next 2,000 years. It was not until the late 1500s that an Italian surgeon described how he repaired torn noses.

In Gaspare Tagliacozzi's time, **duels** were not uncommon. In these showdowns, angry rivals often faced off with swords. And they ended up with **severed** noses. They came to Tagliacozzi to help restore their faces. The innovative surgeon would cut a flap of skin in the arm of the injured person, but leave it attached. He then formed the flap into the shape of a nose. He attached the new nose to the face, but did not cut it away from the arm.

Dueling often resulted in severed noses and other injuries for participants.

His patient spent the next two weeks in great discomfort, his arm pressed against his face. Finally, the flap was cut free of the arm, and the patient returned to normal life.

The transplants that took place in India and Italy were alike in some ways. They both involved using the patient's own skin. It is likely that many of these people survived.

In years to come, more daring transplants took place. Over the next three centuries, doctors took tissues and organs from patients' relatives, from strangers, and even from animals. Then they transplanted them into their ill patients.

In the early 1900s, surgeons across Europe were transplanting goat, sheep, rabbit, pig, and monkey tissues into humans. Others were attempting transplants using tissues and organs from **cadavers**. Their operations always failed. Many people wondered whether doctors should attempt these kinds of transplants.

With all their experimentation, scientists began to realize something. When tissues were cut away and then transplanted to the same person, that person might survive. When animal and cadaver organs were transplanted to people, the patients were certain to die. Somehow, the human body "knew" which tissues were its own, and it accepted them. It also recognized **foreign** tissues and rejected them.

 In 1818, a book titled *Frankenstein, or The Modern Prometheus,* appeared in print. The book was written by a young author named Mary Shelley. It tells the tale of Dr. Frankenstein, a scientist who creates a human being from body parts of the dead. Although he intends to develop something beautiful, things do not turn out that way. His creature looks horrible and does terrible things.

Frankenstein was printed at a time when there were many advances in science. In fact, some people worried that science was moving ahead too quickly. What might have been Shelley's reason for writing the book?

In about 1901, Karl Landsteiner, a Viennese doctor, appeared on the scene. Landsteiner had studied chemistry and medicine. He knew that problems sometimes occurred when people received blood **transfusions**. While some patients improved after the procedure, others got worse. Landsteiner thought he knew what was happening, so he tried some experiments.

Landsteiner mixed blood samples from different pairs of people. He noted that sometimes the mixed blood formed clumps and sometimes it did not. Later, he showed that there were four different types of human blood (A, B, AB, and O). He also showed that transfusions between people with the same types worked out fine. The blood did not clump.

This discovery was important to people having blood transfusions. In time it would also prove to be important to those having organ transplants.

Karl Landsteiner made important discoveries about blood types.

Meanwhile, other scientists were making important discoveries. The Russian scientist Ilya Mechnikov found that animal tissues could protect themselves against foreign substances. And Paul Ehrlich of Germany was figuring out exactly how they did this.

The discoveries of Landsteiner, Mechnikov, and Ehrlich changed everything. Over the next 100 years, the science of transplantation grew. And more and more patients survived.

CHAPTER TWO

# Thinking Small

Throughout most of transplant history, the same problems came up time after time. A surgeon would transplant a monkey's organ into a human, and the patient would die. Another doctor would place a sheep's organ into a human, and the patient would die. Another would try a pig's organ or a dog's organ, always with the same disappointing result.

It was difficult for scientists to see why animal organs failed in human patients. After all, the organs came from perfectly healthy animals. They functioned just fine—until they were transplanted. It was even more difficult to understand why transplants using organs from cadavers failed. These were human organs, and they didn't work either. What was the problem?

Some early transplant attempts used organs from sheep and placed them in human bodies. These transplants were not successful.

The problem was that few doctors or scientists were thinking small enough. They were thinking only of the organs themselves. They were not thinking of what happened to cells after a transplant. Cells are the smallest units that make up tissues and organs. Most cells can be seen only with a microscope, but they have quite active lives. In the early 1900s, very few people were studying these tiny structures.

But Ilya Mechnikov and Paul Ehrlich were. Mechnikov worked with **larval** sea stars. He noticed cells that seemed to protect the sea star from foreign substances. His work led him to believe that many animals had cells that fought invaders.

Paul Ehrlich (above) shared the 1908 Nobel Prize in Medicine with Ilya Mechnikov.

Still, there was much to learn. Someone needed to think even smaller, and that's exactly what Ehrlich was doing. He was in Germany studying cells. In particular, he was looking at the outside surface of cells. He believed that the cell surfaces were covered with large, complex **molecules**. Ehrlich thought these molecules trapped nutrients to feed the cell.

When Ehrlich came out with his ideas, some scientists thought he had lost his mind. Others, however, thought he was on to something. Either way, his ideas prompted many scientists to take a closer look at cell surfaces.

Over time, some of Ehrlich's ideas were proven true. But others were not. Researchers found that cells do have large molecules on their surfaces. In fact, every person has his or her own specific set of molecules. Those molecules are on cell surfaces throughout the body. Scientists also found that special white blood cells circulate in the blood. These white cells—or **lymphocytes**—constantly "look at" the large molecules on cell surfaces. They recognize

## Learning & Innovation Skills

For centuries, patients always died after receiving the organs of animals or cadavers. But when they had skin transplants using their own skin, they often lived. What was unique about their own tissues that allowed patients to live after a skin transplant? Why didn't their bodies reject that skin tissue? Why do you think it took scientists so long to figure this out?

the molecules that belong in their own body. They also recognize surface molecules that come from somewhere else. They attack these foreign molecules as soon as they see them.

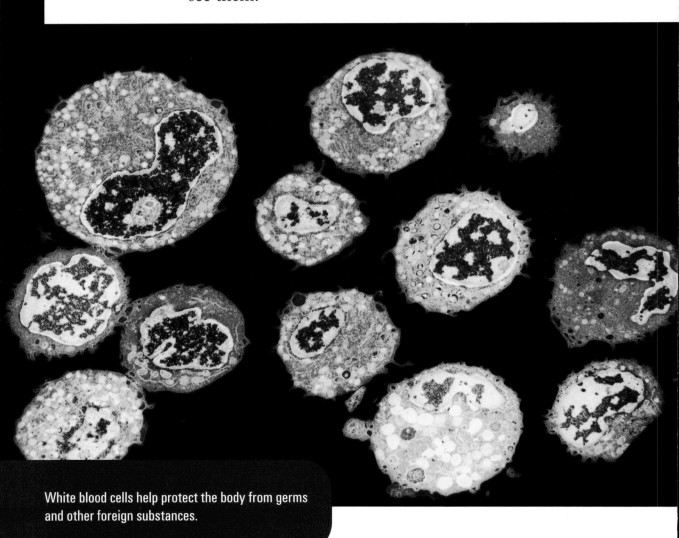

White blood cells help protect the body from germs and other foreign substances.

This information is just what transplant experts needed to jump-start the problem-solving process. The problems they kept running into had nothing to do with the health of the organs themselves. The problems had to do with cells that made up those organs.

Transplanted organs were made up of cells that had their very own surface molecules. When those organs went into **recipients**, the recipients' lymphocytes went wild. They "knew" that these surface molecules were not from their own body—they came from outside. The lymphocytes attacked the transplanted organs. This made it impossible for them to function. So the organ recipients always died.

The scientists and doctors needed all of this information. It explained why transplants were not working. But still, they thought, there must be a way around this problem. Could those lymphocytes be tricked? Could they be forced to ignore invaders?

CHAPTER THREE

# How to Fool a Cell

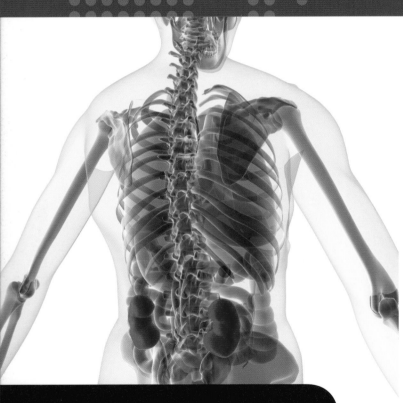

People have two kidneys. That is why it is possible for someone to donate a kidney to another person whose kidneys aren't working.

In 1954, a doctor in Boston, Massachusetts, performed an unusual kidney transplant. He did not use a kidney from an animal or from a cadaver. Instead, he took one kidney from a young, healthy man and put it into his sick twin brother.

A week later, the recipient was still alive. A month later, he was just fine. In fact, he lived eight more years after his transplant. How was this possible? Why didn't his lymphocytes attack the new kidney? Why didn't they spot the surface molecules of that organ?

The lymphocytes had been tricked. The donor and recipient were identical twins. They not only looked alike, but even their blood and cells were alike. They had the same blood type, so their blood would not clump when mixed. They also had exactly the same molecules on their cell surfaces. To the recipient's lymphocytes, the donor kidney cells looked just like the rest of the body cells. So they did not attack the kidney. The transplant was a tremendous success!

Even a success story can make scientists ask more questions. Would transplants between other family members work just as well? Would transplants between distant cousins work?

Scientists compared the cells of family members. They studied the large molecules on their cell surfaces. They saw that, among brothers and sisters, there was a chance that two **siblings** would have identical molecules. A transplant between those siblings would have a good chance of success.

Classifying the cell surfaces of donors and recipients is called tissue typing. Figuring out their blood groups is called blood typing. When the blood and tissues of a donor match those of a recipient, a transplant

is more likely to work. The patient has a greater chance of surviving.

Unfortunately, it is not always possible to find the perfect match. Doctors do not want to put their patients through operations if the chances of survival are low. So they began to wonder if there was a way to **suppress** the lymphocytes.

Then in 1972, **cyclosporine** was discovered. Cyclosporine is a chemical that is produced by a fungus. It has certain qualities that made scientists think it might affect lymphocytes. They thought it might even stop lymphocytes from attacking foreign tissues. If that were true, cyclosporine could really help transplant patients. It was worth a try.

In 1978, cyclosporine was given to some patients who had just received new kidneys. The chemical did a remarkable job. It stopped the patients' lymphocytes from attacking the new organs. Cyclosporine was an exciting discovery for everyone awaiting a transplant.

Another tricky step in organ transplantation is keeping the organ functioning when it is not in a body. Normally, the organ would stop functioning soon after it was removed from a donor. Often the organ being

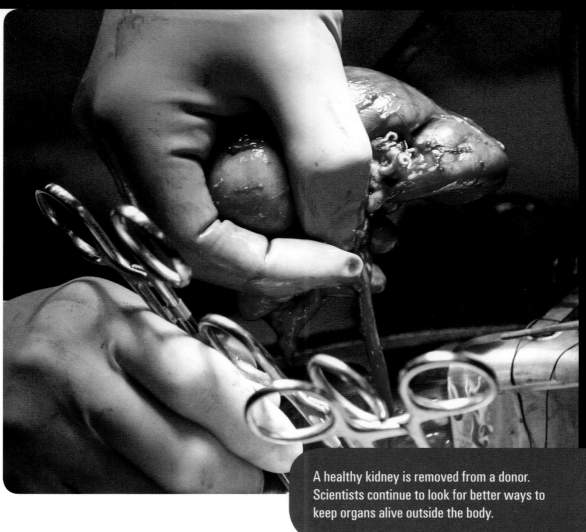

A healthy kidney is removed from a donor. Scientists continue to look for better ways to keep organs alive outside the body.

donated is far away from the recipient. Scientists have found ways to keep organs alive longer outside the body. The longer an organ is kept alive and healthy, the farther it can travel. Researchers continue to look for ways to preserve organs outside the body for longer periods of time.

CHAPTER FOUR

# Transplants of the Future

**R**ight now, there are many people who need a transplant to stay alive. Thousands of patients have diseased lungs, hearts, kidneys, livers, and other organs. They are waiting for healthy organs to become available to them.

The organs usually come from people who have died and who have agreed to donate them. These organs must match the blood and tissue types of the recipients. There are fewer people who choose to donate their organs after death than there are people who need transplants. So the waiting list for organ transplants is quite long.

The long waiting list is forcing scientists to come up with new ideas. Some believe that animal organs might be used in the future. Maybe the animals could

Many people complete organ donor registration forms, but there are still long waiting lists for transplants.

be medically treated so their organs would be safe to transplant into humans.

Other scientists think it might be better to implant electrical devices into humans. After all, heart patients have implanted devices to regulate their heartbeats. Perhaps other organs could be assisted by machines.

## 21st Century Content

**Scientists are working on better drugs to give to transplant patients. In addition to cyclosporine, they have found several other good drugs. These all help the body to accept an organ, but they can damage the body in other ways. Scientists would like to find the perfect drug, but that discovery seems far away. In the meantime, doctors must continue to weigh the health risks and health benefits of a drug before using it on a transplant patient.**

Then no one would have to wait for the perfect organ match.

In some labs, scientists are growing sheets of skin tissue from just a few cells. The sheets are applied to people who have been burned. This helps them to heal more quickly. Scientists are now working on ways to grow sheets of many other types of tissue.

In some cases, doctors are using one organ for more than one transplant. The liver, for example, is a very large organ. Doctors have tried cutting one liver in half and transplanting the halves into two patients. Perhaps this could work with certain other organs. Scientists continue to come up with new ideas for transplants.

CHAPTER FIVE

# Giants in the Field

**A** century ago, a transplant meant almost certain death for a patient. Today, transplants give patients longer lives. Many scientists have helped to make this possible.

### Ilya Mechnikov

Ilya Mechnikov was the one who first realized that cells had protective roles. As a young man, Mechnikov was interested

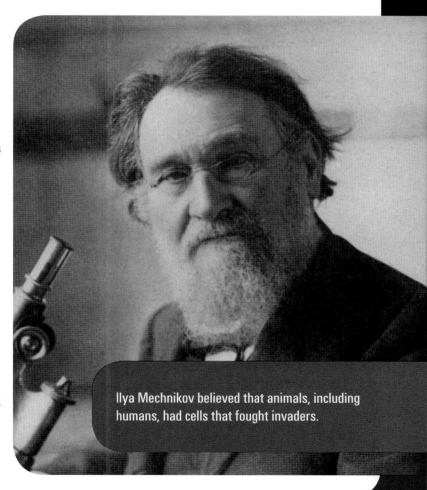

Ilya Mechnikov believed that animals, including humans, had cells that fought invaders.

in marine biology. He was fascinated by the tiny creatures he studied under the microscope. He taught university students in Russia and eventually married. His wife was sickly, though, and died at a young age. Deeply affected by his loss, Mechnikov tried to take his own life.

Fortunately, he was unsuccessful. He married again, but his second wife became very ill. Her illness deeply saddened Mechnikov. He again attempted, unsuccessfully, to end his life. Soon he left his university job. He set up his own lab and began studying sea star **larvae**.

One day, he noticed certain cells moving inside the sea star's body. They reminded him of some cells that existed in more complex animals. Those cells escaped from blood vessels during infections and moved around the body. Could these sea star cells also have something to do with infection?

Mechnikov tried an experiment. He got some thorns from a Christmas decoration and brought them into his lab. He placed them inside the body of a young sea star. The next day, he saw the thorns completely surrounded by those **mobile** cells. Perhaps, he thought, those cells were protecting the sea star. Maybe they destroyed germs that entered the sea star's body. And maybe the escaping blood cells in more complex animals did the same thing.

This is an adult sea star. Mechnikov tested his ideas on young sea stars that weren't fully developed.

Mechnikov tried similar experiments in other animals. Over and over, he saw the same thing. Animals actually had cells that protected them! This discovery turned Mechnikov's life around. His sadness lifted, and he found new excitement in his work. In 1908, he and Paul Ehrlich won the Nobel Prize for their work with cells.

### Alexis Carrel

While some scientists were busy studying cells, at least one was looking at transplants in another way. This was Alexis Carrel. Dr. Carrel worked in France. During

Alexis Carrel was born in France in 1873.

World War I (1914–1918), he served as an army doctor. He treated many wounded soldiers.

Carrel was interested in developing better transplant techniques. In particular, he hoped to find a good way to sew blood vessels together. In his day, doctors used poor methods to stitch up wounds. Sometimes, the patients bled to death despite their stitches.

Carrel had noticed that his mother was excellent at embroidery. This is a type of sewing in which tiny needles are used to make fine, delicate stitches. Carrel decided that the same fine stitches might work to sew blood vessels together during transplants. Using thin silk thread and tiny needles, he practiced stitching paper. Soon he tried his hand with a patient. His work was a success. It added greatly to the art of transplantation.

Carrel did not stop there. He also discovered that tissues awaiting transplants should be kept in cold storage. This kept the tissues in good shape for longer periods of time. In 1912, he won the Nobel Prize for his work.

Joseph Murray won the Nobel Prize for Medicine in 1990.

## Joseph Murray

Another pioneer is Joseph Murray. Dr. Murray was the surgeon in Boston who operated on the identical twins. When he began the kidney transplant, he had no idea he was making history. "We didn't even think of history," he says. "We thought we were going to save a patient."

At the time, Murray thought that transplants did not have much future. He thought they might help only a few people. Little did he know that over the next 60 years, transplants would save hundreds of thousands of lives.

### Life & Career Skills

Before the 1954 operation on the twins, their doctors considered many things. In fact, they wondered if the transplant was even the right thing to do. This would be the first time that a perfectly healthy person would undergo an operation that would not benefit him in any way. The healthy twin might not survive the surgery. Or he might have medical problems for the rest of his life. The doctors sought the advice of many people before making their decision. They talked with other physicians, religious leaders of many faiths, and lawyers. In the end, they decided to perform the transplant, and both twins survived.

# Glossary

**cadavers** (kuh-DA-vurz) dead human bodies

**cyclosporine** (sy-kluh-SPOR-een) a chemical produced by a fungus; it was later given to transplant patients to reduce organ rejection

**duels** (DOO-ulz) contests fought between two people with deadly weapons

**foreign** (FOR-ehn) coming from another place

**larvae** (LAR-vee) the young, undeveloped forms of some animals

**larval** (LAR-vuhl) having to do with larvae

**lymphocytes** (LIM-fuh-syts) white blood cells that recognize the surface molecules of other cells as either foreign or not

**mobile** (MO-buhl) moving around

**molecules** (MAH-lih-kyoolz) extremely small structures made up of atoms

**mutilation** (myoo-tuh-LAY-shun) damage caused by injury or the removal of something

**recipients** (rih-SIH-pee-uhnts) people who receive something

**severed** (SEH-vurd) completely cut off

**siblings** (SIH-bleengz) brothers and sisters

**suppress** (suh-PRESS) to slow down or stop the activity of something

**tissues** (TIH-shyooz) masses of cells that form a particular part of a plant or animal

**transfusions** (tranz-FYOO-zhunz) the act of transferring blood or another liquid into the blood vessels of a person

# For More Information

## BOOKS

Ballard, Carol. *Cutting Edge Medicine: Organ Transplants*. Milwaukee, WI: World Almanac Library, 2007.

Barter, James. *Great Medical Discoveries: Organ Transplants*. Farmington Hills, MI: Lucent Books, 2006.

Farndon, John. *From Laughing Gas to Face Transplants: Discovering Transplant Surgery*. Chicago: Heinemann Library, 2006.

## WEB SITES

Enchanted Learning
*www.enchantedlearning.com/subjects/anatomy/titlepage.shtml*
Visit to learn more about basic human anatomy

Transplant Kids
*www.transplantkids.co.uk/info.html*
Information for children who are expecting to have a transplant

Transplant Living
*www.transplantliving.org/SharedContentDocuments/Childrens_Brochure(1).pdf*
A brochure explaining what children might expect of a transplant

# Index

## About the Author

Susan H. Gray has a master's degree in zoology. She has taught college-level courses in biology, anatomy, and physiology. She has also written more than 90 science and reference books for children. In her free time, she likes to garden and play the piano. Susan lives in Cabot, Arkansas, with her husband, Michael, and many pets.